DREAM OF THE BIRD TATTOO

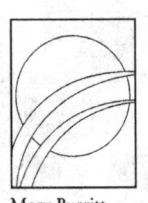

Mary Burritt Christiansen Poetry Series
Hilda Raz, Series Editor

Mary Burritt
Christiansen
Poetry Series

The Mary Burritt Christiansen Poetry Series publishes
two to four books a year that engage and give voice
to the realities of living, working, and experiencing
the West and the Border as places and as metaphors.
The purpose of the series is to expand access to, and the audience for,
quality poetry, both single volumes and anthologies, that can be used
for general reading as well as in classrooms.

Also available in the Mary Burritt Christiansen Poetry Series:

A Real Man Would Have a Gun: Poems by Stacey Waite
Unruly Tree: Poems by Leslie Ullman
A Walk with Frank O'Hara: Poems by Susan Aizenberg
Light of Wings: Poems by Sarah Kotchian
Trials and Tribulations of Dirty Shame, Oklahoma: And Other Prose Poems
    by Sy Hoahwah
A Guide to Tongue Tie Surgery: Poems by Tina Carlson
Point of Entry: Poems by Katherine DiBella Seluja
Victory Garden: Poems by Glenna Berry Horton Luschei
Suggest Paradise: Poems by Ray Gonzalez
Reflections through the Convex Mirror of Time / Reflexiones tras el Espejo
    Convexo del Tiempo: Poems in Remembrance of the Spanish Civil War /
    Poemas en Recuerdo de la Guerra Civil Española by E. A. Mares

For additional titles in the Mary Burritt Christiansen Poetry Series,
please visit unmpress.com.

Dream of the Bird Tattoo

POEMS AND SUEÑITOS

JUAN J. MORALES

UNIVERSITY OF NEW MEXICO PRESS | ALBUQUERQUE

Library of Congress Cataloging-in-Publication Data
Names: Morales, Juan J., author. Title: Dream of the bird tattoo:
poems and sueñitos / Juan J. Morales. Other titles: Dream
of the bird tattoo (Compilation) | Mary Burritt Christiansen
poetry series.
Description: Albuquerque: University of New Mexico Press,
2025. | Series: Mary Burritt Christiansen poetry series
Identifiers: LCCN 2024028954 (print) | LCCN 2024028955
(ebook) | ISBN 9780826367587 (paperback) |
ISBN 9780826367594 (epub)
Subjects: LCGFT: Poetry.
Classification: LCC PS3613.O7155 D74 2025 (print) |
LCC PS3613.O7155 (ebook) | DDC 811/.6—dc23/eng/20240812
LC record available at https://lccn.loc.gov/2024028954
LC ebook record available at https://lccn.loc.gov/2024028955

Founded in 1889, the University of New Mexico sits on the
traditional homelands of the Pueblo of Sandia. The original
peoples of New Mexico—Pueblo, Navajo, and Apache—since
time immemorial have deep connections to the land and have
made significant contributions to the broader community
statewide. We honor the land itself and those who remain
stewards of this land throughout the generations and also
acknowledge our committed relationship to Indigenous peoples.
We gratefully recognize our history.

Cover illustration and interior
illustrations courtesy of Design Cuts
Designed by Felicia Cedillos
Composed in Chaparral Pro

IN MEMORIAM

Jose Morales Lugo
April 19, 1932–February 2, 2019

Contents

Of Avocados

Like two hands pressed
together, they are twice as large
on the island. One feeds
the family meal, sending us to wonder,
Why are they so small
stateside? On our last visit to PR
we sat on my tío's patio
to talk and drink cafecitos.
My dad stared down the giant tree
burdened with dark green fruit.
His brother didn't offer him
a single one.
My tío died soon after.
Dad kept bringing up
the abundance his brother never offered,
not as a grudge, but as a recollection
of what we still couldn't get in the States,
of what was delicious enough
to keep all borders open.
Within the year two more
of Dad's siblings passed away,
and last week we lost him,
a man who planned to return for
one more avocado. For each of us
he would have peeled away craggy skin,

parsed flesh, and held out
those green wedges
on his knife's point. We would have
accepted it
as one last gift
to savor.

Life Support

*On a bleary-eyed morning, after two and a half hours of sleep, I swapped Facebook messages with cousins in PR. I told them my father was on his way to the crossroads, passing on, and other euphemisms to avoid saying he was going to die.

*Waiting for family to arrive for goodbyes, I sent everyone a photo of Dad's tattoo, and we talked about getting it in his honor, instead of all other arrangements.

*I played phone tag with the Purple Heart, VFW, and retirees until we secured our father's military honors. Whenever they gave me condolences, I wanted to tell them, "Not yet."

*My work friend texted me a question and then insisted on bringing us soup. My first spoonful interrupted my overlooked hunger because I was feeling so gnawed up inside.

*On speakerphone in the ICU, my tío told me in Spanish that he was a rock rooted in the river for me to hold on to. I hoped I translated it correctly and wondered if Dad could hear his brother's voice.

*My niece asked about making plaster handprints so the kids, who weren't kids anymore, could hold abuelito's hard-working hands. I told her about the first day in the ICU when he rested in bed, eyes closed, hands held up to the afterlife.

*At the end of a night when I didn't sleep in the hospital, my sister texted two hearts. I replied, "I love you too."

*Thursday night, when we took him off life support, the whole family surrounded him, and I held his hand, telling him it's okay to go. In English, Spanish, and tears, I promised to tell his story. He held on for two more days.

*At the end of the week my brother sent me the hospice care rep's name, telling me to leave a message.

*Whenever asked how, we explained what must have been a fall during his morning walk. We only knew bleeding and damage pointed out on the scans. The remaining questions swirled around his empty hospital bed on Saturday morning.

My Father's Blasphemy, or Excerpt from *Shit My Puerto Rican Father Said*

*

It is music that spits in the face of the church, adding shit, whores, leaven bread, and classic f-bombs. We know it better than any scripture. My sisters, brother, and I quote him with the same pauses and emphasis that taught us you can't always hold compassion in your heart. Sometimes you must tell the insurance agent, who just raised your premiums, "I might be a little man, but I will stomp your ass all over this parking lot."

Dream of the Space Tattoo

Inside a dream within a dream, my dad sits next to me, telling me about his new tattoo. I lift his sleeve and look at his left shoulder. Instead of the faded green bird there is a fresh spaceship, housed in a vertical rectangle. The nose of the ship is outlined in black and colored with brilliant reds and yellows. Where there should be white is his flesh. Toward the bottom I study the Roman numeral XI and celestial coordinates telling us where to meet. My mind is traveling galaxies and dark frontiers through overheard whispers of time travel. I'm crying because I lost him four months ago, and I wake up repeating, "He knows where we have to go." Everyone in the room pauses conversations to look at me. I'm pointing to my vanishing father, still poking at his tattoo.

Lost Photo of Pop Holding an Anaconda

The last time I touched
the black-and-white photo
was in middle school,
assembling a
family tree for Spanish class.
I worry I was the one
who lost it. Mom promises
I returned it, but I search
closets and boxes,
flip through yearbooks, and
open crowded drawers
to see if I find you
standing in the middle,
beaming a smile,
and a head shorter than
the ten other men.
You all hold the anaconda,
thick as a muscular tree trunk
and thirty feet long,
in front of the Canal Zone's
dense jungle. I describe it now,
hoping to chance upon
you while snooping
and cleaning at Mom's house.
If the photo is
really lost, I will resume
searching until
I can consider it,
like you,
never truly lost.

My Father's War Medals

My brother sorts them
in an oak shadowbox
surrounding our Pop's
sergeant major patch.
Pinned on a black background,
ordered by distinction,
left to right, three rows—
Bronze Star, Purple Heart,
Medal of Valor,
Legion of Merit,
Army Commendation, and ten more.
Stripes and colors
tell his histories.
The polished medals form
a glowing field, war flowers,
understated, like his tombstone—
cross, favorite psalm, and will to serve.
My brother leaves out
the duplicates and triplicates
and sighs.

Excerpt from
Shit My Puerto Rican Father Said

---

*

When my dad's knee swelled up from embedded grenade
shrapnel from the Korean War, Mom wouldn't let him mow
the lawn. He argued his case: "The doctor don't give a shit if
I cut the grass or if I set it on fire." The compromise was him
supervising, me mowing, and her watching him not mow.
Whenever she went inside he took the mower away to cut a row
of grass before giving it back to me. I tried to cover for him by
mimicking his style and form.

The Waves, or Las Olas

*

The waves, the waves
the waves, the waves

On the beach, South Padre Island, rough waves
overlap, rise, fall, tumble, and I understand
something new. The fog lifts from the day before
and pelicans continue formations above.
It is now blue as the sun severs clouds like a wound
I try to rush past. Waves hit my bare feet,
colder than expected. For a moment I forget
we lost dad almost a month ago. It rushes and presses me
weak inside, even though I know it will
eventually heal. Ebb and flow. Some waves crash harder
than others. I regret forgetting his voice
and all questions I thought I still had time to ask.
My father gives me everything, buried
somewhere in infinite grains of sand.

*

The waves, the waves
the waves, las olas

Some questions will resolve by adapting
to the cold water. Then, I will step back
onto the dry sand that clings to my feet.
I listen again to the crash and forth continue,
almost roaring. I will do my best to board
the plane home and tell his story. I will survive
even though I will never get over
the military cemetery with a small marker
waiting for the permanent tombstone's arrival.
I will learn what else I have to ask, standing over
him in the eastward plains of Colorado. I will return
to say what I am too afraid to repeat—the goodbye
that flowed out of me, as if I were
talking in tongues, weeks ago in the ICU.

*

The waves, the waves
las olas, the waves

*

The waves, the waves
las olas, las olas

The ocean glides over the sand, cresting
then receding like water off
a duck's back. His heart rate
floats away, adrift, out to sea
all over again. The heartbreak eases
to shore, tangled with the clumps
of seaweed and debris from
spring breakers and snowbirds
that litter the picturesque beaches.
The blue jellyfish fragments
are landmines that sting to the bone,
lasting longer than footprints
and the sand castles that are
built to fight but always fall away.

*

The waves, las olas
the waves, the waves

Even though he was born on an island, my father
grew up content in the rugged mountainside.
He was Boricua, a word derived from
the Taíno word "Boriken," meaning "land of brave lords."
He was also content in the snow, la nieve that melts
into streams and creeks, reunites in rivers,
greets the sea, and merges back into the waves.
Las olas, they suddenly tumble over me. I am stunned
with sea foam. They crash louder but leave room
for contemplation—kissing my father's hand, hugging
him after a peaceful Sunday together
that felt somehow perfect, like his pressed
uniform dry-cleaned and hanging in his closet
and all his military papers organized on the basement desk.

*

The waves, las olas
the waves, las olas

*

The waves, las olas
las olas, the waves

The waves rolling through my head, just like
the mantra "poco a poco" that Mom already taught me.
It helps plant my feet even when sand recedes beneath
my heels, water always stealing away the grains.
She's always gifting me Spanish words over the phone
and teasing me when she says, "Mommy knows best."
The last time we spoke, she swore she heard
Dad sneezing from the afterlife. Her voice defeated.
When I told my mom she is strong even when
she doesn't feel it, I was also speaking to myself.
Thinking of her, back home and interrupting the silence with
Caso Cerrado or a favorite ghost show on Netflix,
I am standing on the shoreline with lapping olas,
ready for them to welcome or knock me down.

*

The waves, las olas
las olas, las olas

After a week of hospital visits on burned-out
slivers of sleep that ignored the world outside
of my father's ICU room, I went to yoga,
forty miles away, back in Pueblo. I quieted,
struggled to meet form, and cried through
the poses. With eyes shut I felt the long rope
that bound me to my father. It untethered and fell away
to black space. It hurt to unburden—a sunset,
an inarticulate slump of giving body
to exhaustion, a sigh to release for my father
no longer in pain. A few minutes later, outside
the yoga studio, my brother called to tell me
our father slipped away while everyone
in the hospital room conversed. Gone.

*

Las olas, the waves
the waves, the waves

Sometimes I wear memories splashed like the reek
of machismo and sting of aftershave.
I breathe deep in the limo, recalling my father's scent
on the way to the cemetery. Thinking it his ghost
until realizing the driver wore the same Old Spice
that Pop tapped on his neck to end the ritual
of a shower and shave. Men of their generation loved
the soapy shaving brush, followed by the slow, straight shave
and neatly trimmed mustache, promptly
washing away the stink of a double or after
toiling in the yard. Sometimes a blunt blow of grief
stabs me at day's end with work clothes peeled off
and thrown into the hamper. I hold back tears
meant to be shed, pushing myself to shut down.

Las olas, las olas
las olas, las olas

The stars and stripes draped over
the casket. The unwavering flag in the wind.
The arranged flowers around the gunmetal casket
matched the red, white, and blue flag,
which two soldiers folded after the 21-gun salute,
while the bugler faced away, due west, toward
the purple mountain majesty above the city.
Tava, the Mountain of the Sun,
housed an excess of snowcap, and they worked the flag
into a slow triangle, tucked between each step
with white-gloved hands. The ranking officer stowed
shell casings into the flag and delivered it
into my mother's hands. We wept together,
knowing Pop would call the service perfect.

Las olas, the waves
las olas, the waves

*

Las olas, the waves
las olas, las olas

It's not an original conceit or metaphor
when my therapist reminded me that grief
manifests as the waves. I've heard it on TV shows
when they kill off characters, but it's different
swimming up as carried guilt whenever I laugh
or erupt in anger. It's okay that last week I shook
the vending machine for dispensing the wrong candy bar,
outside the ICU. When my therapist tried
to take me further than five stages, I resisted.
We settled on me accepting the ever-changing order.
I left her office, still trapped in a riptide.
I tried to forgive myself whenever
bitterness overtook the gratitude within.
Stay afloat and find your way back to shore.

*

Las olas, las olas
the waves, the waves

I confess to secret moments when I feel
embarrassed for taking this so hard.
Back when I got divorced, my father said,
"You are not the first; you will not be the last."
It balanced out my devastated mother
who took the news harder than me, seeing me as
a destroyed high schooler, always heartbroken
by what I naively assumed to be love. Afterward,
we went off-kilter with the lost father—
who led our family prayer, joked that one day
he'd become a Walmart greeter or a pastor
of his own damn church, and was the single voice
strong enough to tell us the world
isn't always collapsing, even if it is right now.

*

Las olas, las olas
the waves, las olas

After our cousin's late arrival from Ecuador,
we took Dad off life support, assuming he'd go instantly.
We gathered to tell him he could rest now.
It had been days since he fought to remove his IVs,
mumbled favorite cuss words, lifted hands above his head,
and gave us glimmers of hope. He dreamed and we took turns,
whispering and holding his hand, noticing a firm grip.
We studied his bird tattoos, shrapnel wounds, bites of skin cancer
from Agent Orange. When it was my turn I held on through
the waves of Spanish and English as they came,
promising we'd be okay, promising it was okay to go,
and promising we would never forget. We waited
until late into battered night when we decided
who would go home and who would keep vigil.

*

Las olas, las olas
las olas, the waves

*

Las olas, las olas
las olas, las olas

On Memorial Day my sister, mom, and brother-in-law
are going to the cemetery for the military
ceremony. They will also leave flowers for Pop.
I want to go too, but I can't bring myself
to stand through the military brass salutes
and somber flags at half-mast. I thought I could,
but I'm here writing about the waves, las olas,
feeling guilty because Mom hurts a little more
after each visit. Just like I do with her, I promise Dad
I'm coming to visit on a quieter day,
when I can hear myself speak gratitude and love,
a private ceremony that I wish I could hold
for him every day that dives me deeper than grief
and into the sea full of its waves and olas.

Dream of the Rising Sea

I walk between two loose narratives, connected by a seaside
promenade. Rising from dark water, childhood's plastic toys
and adulthood's kitchen utensils float near the stony edge. I
can't resist gathering anything within reach with promises to
use them in my new life. I ignore my drowning sneakers. Lost
in object memories, I watch sentimentals bubble up, begging
for rescue. A favorite shirt billows to life in the current. By
the time the waves grab my knees, I struggle to release my
unneeded things. When I understand the sea won't stop eating
the land, I skim the surface, now adrift with tarot cards. The
promenade is gone, so I swim the sea, reaching toward higher
ground.

Teaching Me to Shoot Pool

We placed our quarters on the table
        and racked, alternating solids and stripes
in the triangle, middling the eight ball.
        He always let me break, cue ball right of center,
two deep breaths, and crack!

A good break meant spreading the balls as
            a brief solar system on green felt,
      crashed together with planets dropping
into black holes. I would shoot with Pop studying me—
chalk cue, point stick to pocket,
          calculate angles, aim cue ball, and strike.
      We took turns and his tricks taught me to fiercely play
        because he never took it easy on me.
      Banks off rails, scratches, jump shots, English, and luck

kept it interesting. "Working the table," he called it
      when it went right, when the echoed clack
sent the ball gently rolling and then sinking.
      Whenever I tried to muscle
instead of finesse it, I usually missed.

      My Dad then said, "Oh, Papo, now you won't
take another shot" before he'd clean the table.
      After the eight ball found called pocket,
winner always took their time to sink the loser's balls.
      When I gave him a run for his money, I clapped blue chalk
off my hands and racked again, shaping
      my revenge with geometry. I listened

to memories of pool tourneys
        in the army and late nights throwing
    two or three games until his cocky opponent
would ask, "Double or nothing?"
    Unspoken between sips from sweaty Coca-Colas

      and when we were almost out of quarters,
Dad would point to a pocket and I'd catch
    the ball before it vanished
into the pocket. The word "shark" swam
    in my mind and seemed to light up
the dim pool hall, just like his quick wink.

The Fifth Commandment

Every time Mom wanted to cuss
she'd say "chuleta con papas"
or "miércoles" instead
of the swear words my dad muttered
toward the heart of the matter.

Pork chops, potatoes, and Wednesdays
were her musical equivalent to
the "oh shit" or "dammit" she felt
but never said. Meanwhile, Dad
would corral cuss words

from every cardinal direction. When he would lose
his reading glasses, he'd exclaim,
"Where is that piece of shit?"
Mom surprised us with her calm,
"I don't know where you left

that piece of shit." I always gasped,
"Mom!" in response. In my dad's most
flustered moments, we joked
about his ears turning red, white,
and then imagined shooting steam

like a cartoon kettle
until Mom somehow
walked into his storms to defuse unfurling
anger. She always calmed the room,
and I learned to honor

Mother and Father,
as profanity balanced
between the wrath to gently let go
and the cuss words meant
to dance out of my mouth.

The Lighthouse Dream

My father is having a heart attack at the top of the lighthouse,
and I must save him. In my mind, where my waking hovers,
a voice is telling me, "We've already lost him." I'm crying, in
denial, and rushing up the coiling staircase. I unlock the large
door by turning a huge wheel to depressurize the room. The
door hisses open to where my dad rests in a hospital bed, in
the shadow of the giant lens and lantern. I pick him up and
he clings around my neck. The top of the lighthouse opens to
a street full of people, reaching down to carry him to safety.
Sobbing and refusing their help, I bring my father up and onto
the peaceful street. Once he is protected, the voice wakes me
back into the night.

"Puerto Rico Goes Dark"

—*The New York Times*, September 20, 2017

As dark as the busy signal my father gets when calling his
brothers and sister on the southwest part of the island.

As the 95 percent of electricity blinking, then shutting off.

As the empty grocery aisles where they used to store water,
bread, milk, and cereal.

As the unanswered Facebook messages to my primos.

As the colonial Jones Act in place, longer than a century, lifted
for only ten days.

As Pitbull's private plane flies back and forth to deliver the
goods for the people.

As the money sent to them on PayPal with receipts proving
they only bought items on the survival list.

As the familia having a BBQ to use up what will spoil and what
has to be cooked right now.

As the swirl of the storm's eye we watch from the mainland,
thick red circle consuming the entire island under the name
Maria, Category 4.

As the people who would fight about to kneel or not to kneel in
the NFL.

As the people who don't understand PR is a commonwealth, its residents powerless US citizens.

As the four major airlines willing to gouge a plane ticket up to $1,600, $1,800, and $2,000.

As me posting more prayers for PR, with a handful of likes.

As El Yunque's trees splintered and thrown into the void.

As the Boricuas who hike each Saturday to the crossroad, near the last standing cell tower, making phone calls to the list of people from town until the signal goes out again.

As someone's sarcasm, saying, "For once I'm glad I have AT&T."

As the devastated ports, tangled full of boats trying to deliver supplies.

As the decade's worth of infrastructure that needed updating long ago, all washed away.

As smaller Caribbean islands, wiped out.

As helpless as someone making plans to donate blood next week.

As my father again, assuming everyone okay, but needing to hear from anyone.

As the San Juan airport down to a handful of functioning gates.

As the thickest miles of trees now a flat, unobstructed view of the favorite beach.

As Mexico City after its earthquake last week, and Houston and Harvey a few weeks before.

As a still-hidden gem the world doesn't visit.

As exhausted as Jorge, here in Pueblo, on the phone with everyone except his father, who is helping to clean up the neighborhood.

As me, finally becoming speechless for once.

As the flicker of hospital generators running on diesel.

As the president complaining that "these people want everything done for them."

As the complexion of the people, making them less important to the government.

As the hole where the coquis still whistle.

As the quick phone call from a prima who tells me they're okay and then asks, "Where do we start to rebuild?"

As the news broadcasts moving on to talk about the rest of the world in the dark.

Dogma

I paid twenty bucks for a white T-shirt
at a Nine Inch Nails concert when I was fifteen.
At the center a medieval demon framed
its hands around the band's name in red.
Like an illumination, the demon wore crooked wings.
Before I could wear my satanic shirt, my mom scolded me
for bringing the evil home and offered me
forty bucks to burn it. She tricked me into thinking
it was my own idea. I never saw my mom cast it
into hell on our holy barbecue grill, but after school
she declared it gone. I scowled at the Church's hypocrisy
for taking away my shirt and brooded
with elevated angst. My adolescence didn't change much—
I dyed my hair black, kept spinning guttural singers,
slammed myself into mosh pit chaos, and played
violent music videos too loud—
except I stopped carrying the darkness home,
even if it meant walking a few lonely blocks
out of the way to lose it first.

Dream of the Wolf

There's an empty room that belongs only to me. I feel territorial and conflicted with the wolf inside, which is a beautifully sharp creature, always smiling. I'm supposed to keep him cooped up, and he wants out to do some harm. He asks me to admire the long gouges and scratches decorating the walls. He wrestles with me, like an older sibling holding back, so I worry about setting him off. When the wolf bites me too hard, I correct with a loud "No!" I leave him to think about his defiance, and I lock the two red doors before remembering there's also a blue door, slightly ajar. When the wolf escapes, I know I'm responsible. I can smell the coming slaughter, and I'm alone to figure out if the wolf will return and if I left the door open on purpose.

Excerpt from
Shit My Puerto Rican Father Said

*

My father's version of "the talk" happened when I was
seventeen. I was driving, and I remembered the stretch of
Cheyenne Mountain Road just before the movie theater and
shopping center. He turned and asked, "Do you know about
sex?" I answered, "Yes." He concluded the conversation with
"Good. Don't do it." He changed the subject back to silence,
leaving me with what I needed to know.

"Are You Sure This Isn't You?"

Everyone asks. To hold his photo reflects our youth
offended when compared to our parents.
The photo is torn. Whose hand rests around
Pop's shoulder? He dons a garrison cap,
uniform jacket over standard-issue shirt,
a Windsor knot, maybe the same black tie
he used to teach me, decades later. To hold the photo
is to hold our father, to visit him, top left corner
of the vanity's big mirror, in my childhood home's basement.
Our father, soldier in sepia, circa 1952.
My brother swears it had to be after combat
in Korea, evidenced by the rectangular medal
with long rifle on his chest, his collar's gold buttons.
We convene around the photo to discover
his likeness within. We now receive it as praise, catching ourselves
using his mannerisms with delight—
how he cleared his throat and loved to shoot
the breeze with strangers. He carries my resemblance—
smile, nose, eyebrows, and ears, posed in the uncanny invite
to imagine me as his reincarnation,
nearly identical, except for my darker eyes.

Dream of the Old Antique Shop

*

I will be working evenings, but the owner and cowboy regulars don't give me instructions. They tell me I'll keep an eye on things. "Don't be surprised when all this junk moves on its own," one of them snarls. "Like the old puppets in the back, always talking and shambling on the floors. Might help to learn their names." I smirk until the owner fights a floating dress back onto its hanger, but I'm scared with this show of force. Everything smells intriguing, like worn leather and stale tobacco.

*

When I bring you with me after hours, everyone has left for the day except the invisibles. You are creeped out by three giant masks parroting our conversation. A hairpin with peacock feathers winks at you. The other objects clatter to say, "Pick me! Pick me!" Seeing terror on your face, my amusement ends. We guide each other out of the shop, past the aisles of vintage clothes and glass displays full of handprints, cigarette cases, arrowheads, and belt buckles, understanding I would promise not to work here, but we have obligations. The best I can do is never let the lonely souls ever find you again.

The Saddest Song

During my first year of teaching, my class met in a black box theater.
We circled the chairs next to the grand piano. One student always
    arrived
early to play the song, maybe to impress or because he didn't have a
    piano.
He sang like he was alone, his classmates filing in. His voice held a
    melancholy
that latched on to us. "Nobody said it was easy," he sang, eyes closed.
When he finished, he let the piano ring out, smiled big, and joined us.
It was grad school for me. I lived on ulcers, never got enough sleep,
and I kept hearing the song everywhere after that. The saddest song.
It banked all my failings and mistakes. It loitered for years
like a house fire's aftermath. It joined my misery-loves-company
    soundtrack
with other love songs I couldn't hear any more, lost in my brain vault
with boxes of CDs and my hard drive of albums that shaped me.
The song became an empty restaurant I never entered and an
    acquaintance
on the same commute I never acknowledged. In the grocery store
I stumbled into it, humming its verse and chorus. Beat by beat, I
    finally let
the song reenact clashes that scarred and letdowns I survived, so
I could keep walking toward the swell of heavies yet to come.

My Father Looking at Bruegel's
Landscape with the Fall of Icarus

After my talk in the art gallery,
where I projected images of paintings and poems,
my father walked up to Breugel's landscape
to offer me a memory—

"That one with the plow?
I used to do that,
behind our house in Lajas.
Except it wasn't
with a horse.
It was a bull, pushing
forward. I steered
the little wheel there
to guide the blade
into soil, slicing
open the field."

I followed him to where
there was no time for sea, ship, or faded city
on the rocky coast—

"From there I planted the sugar cane seeds.
Drop it in, push the dirt over.
Drop it in, push the dirt over.
Drop it in, push the dirt over."

I entered my father's landscape
that ignored Icarus's splash
with eyes only
for the humid field,
now overgrown by decades
when our family's home
gave way
to a kingdom
of massive bee hives.

Nightmare of a Bear

I'm inside a trailer, watching two drunk neighbors torment
a black bear. One man pokes the bear with a sharp stick and
the other is audacious enough to ride on the bear's shoulders,
clapping time on its head. Their big dog barks and circles. I hear
laughter until the men are suddenly not in control. I wince
when the bear strikes the dog dead. Another swipe and one
man's face is gone. He's screaming until he's not. The other
man falls off the bear, ripped in half. After the bear drops to all
fours and sniffs around the aftermath, it wanders back into the
forest, leaving me behind my window to remember that nature
will never go quietly.

My Papa's Morning Walks

Close to 5:00 a.m. you always found random objects
before B Street woke up, carrying my old hockey stick
that cops considered a weapon
and not your walking stick—

the handle Mom used to make rum cake,
polished army boots in the strip club parking lot,
folded twenties, fifties, hundreds dropped,
and once a roll of quarters, winter gloves and ball caps,

and the 1994 crime scene where a letter bomb
once murdered a neighbor, a few blocks over,
with parts of hands and arm in the street
near the dead man and his wounded wife. It reopened

something in you, the two wars you lived through. I tried to ask more,
and you told me instead about the stray dogs
you scared away and everything else found—
friends and neighbors always smiling to tell you "Hello."

Death Jokes

My dad never flinched when talking about death;
in fact, he roused plans as casual as planting
his garden every spring. From there jokes bloomed as smirks
on his face—

"When I die, I'm going to be buried with my checkbook,
so whenever you spend money, you'll have
to tell me hello." I laughed

and didn't feel fear for
his life ceasing yet. I didn't know the plummet
I would feel inside when I got the call.

He always danced past death to say, "Maria, when you
kick the bucket, I'll lock the door, never answer, and pray
everyone leaves me the hell alone."

In the other version, Dad told us,
"When Mama goes, I'll tie my hammock up to the first
damn trees I find in Puerto Rico."

When death wisecracks back,
it joins you for a sit on the patio
and entices a smile for Dad's death jokes,

nesting like the memory of his backyard
thriving with peach trees and lilacs, in bloom
around empty garden beds,

where he tended to tomatoes, cucumbers, squash,
radishes, and onions until harvest. I imagine him
with another punchline. Remember: It's still okay to laugh.

Visiting Your Grave

I speak to white marble,
marking your name, rank, and wars
at the Pikes Peak National Cemetery.
I read your favorite psalm and a poem
with my family behind me,

waiting in the grass
on a hot morning,
the day after your birthday.
Just before arriving I took a wrong turn
and kept driving

into eastern plains, where
pronghorns tried to tell me something
about quiet. Some grazed and others rested,
blending in yellow grass
under a cloudless sky.

We affirm you would like it here.
Pikes Peak still holds a cap of snow,
and I'm thinking of rivers running
high this summer,
me crying behind sunglasses,

a personal flood. I promise to return soon
with a kiss on top of the tombstone,
like I used to peck
you, my beautiful father, on
your stubbled cheek.

The Veil, or
Dad Checks in with Another Dream

We are walking into a massive building, in a giant city swimming in shapes and traffic. Outside, my father smiles and leans against a pillar. I slap him on his shoulder, and my wife jokes with him, "Uh-oh, looks like this stranger wants to give us trouble." My dad shoots back, "No, no, pretty lady. I came by to make sure everyone is okay." We tell him everything is fine and pause together to take in the metropolis, with all of its fog, light, and shadow, bustling somewhere on that line where the living and the dead have no problem meeting.

Destiny

At the funeral, post pastor, after my eulogy, and before
two speeches from those who didn't know my father well,
my brother-in-law approached the podium,
wearing jeans and his camo biker vest, covered in
combat and POW/MIA patches. I worried
what story about "being in the shit"
might erupt. He steadied himself
and spoke of the time, fifty years ago, when
the river rat met the short-ass Boricua sergeant
on a warship for five minutes in Vietnam. He didn't mention
Pop using R&R to check on a kid from his village
or the story as anecdote, but he continued by calling
our father destiny. Destiny was meeting the father
of the woman he would love and marry in Colorado
years later. Destiny was two hardened men surviving
the hooded executioner they faced in the jungle
so they could compare war wounds at family dinners. Destiny was
my sister telling us our abuelita stood in the hospital hallway,
dressed in black, two nights before she retrieved Pop.
My brother-in-law ended his eulogy with a nod and
sat down, looking forward in complete loss, just like me now,
processing all the coincidences and defied odds
that let them meet across the world and in the heat of war.
Just like him, I have to call it destiny too.

Every Last Supper

I am writing to understand

The Last Supper

    in every childhood home.

How every kitchen table
        centered
        under the painted, carved, or porcelain

        Christ framed by apostles,
            en la cocina,

near the tiny TV
on top of the fridge.

This is still the backdrop
        for crowded meals
            on holidays and

between work
        and school

when our mother cooks.

It is the penitent feeling for never
        wasting bites
        of arroz con lentejas,

and Jesus looking down,

as a relic with opened arms,
        whispering,

"My flesh. My blood.
Eat while you can, mi niño."

El Chupacabra Visits Chicago

I find disappointment in the Midwest—how they keep wanting
me to be Mothman. We both wear red eyes and wings, but
I take no joy in knocking down bridges or their scorching
summertime. Some seem impressed with how much blood
I drink from the throat in one sitting and overlook me as
well-traveled, a fine curator of exquisite dishes, carnally
appreciating the organs of animals I meet.

When it's not Mothman, they mistake me for the gargoyles
in this city, even though most of it burned down almost 150
years ago. Now the city's thrumming more and more Spanish
voices that tempt me to reveal myself. But I know better.
For now I keep hoping I will not always be seen as fear filling
dank alleys and crowding around every uptight skyscraper.
Like a cat gifting dead birds and mice, I'm eager to share the
misunderstood hungers of the world.

Dream of Hungry Crabs

The old man stares into my childhood sandbox, reminiscing about the crabs he caught as a coastal child. Except he calls them cangrejos. He pops bananas open and lays the fruit out on the sand. I wonder how crabs could live so far from sea, and he tells me to have a little faith. I am excited to break cangrejos open and to suck meat from their shells. When the crabs emerge they are brown and wet, clicking joints. Their armored bodies and ravenous hunger terrify me. I feel their claws and legs, like they're scraping pink abrasions onto my skin. They finish the feast, then scamper downward into the folds of sand. I ask the old man, "How can we eat when we didn't catch a single crab?" He laughs like the sea spitting out a whale. Lipping one of the tiny holes with his big toe, he then asks, "How can you still be hungry after that?"

Excerpt from
Shit My Puerto Rican Father Said

*

During a visit home, Father asked me if I wanted a Puerto
Rican omelet. Of course I asked what a Puerto Rican omelet
is, and he answered, "What the hell else am I supposed to call
it when a Puerto Rican makes you an omelet?" He made the
omelet with two types of cheese, ham, bell peppers, tomato,
and leftover arroz. A little later he asked my niece if she wanted
a Puerto Rican omelet.

Dream of the Ladybugs

I speak on a borrowed cell phone in a meadow with tall grass. Nothing makes sense and my voice vanishes on invisible lines to reach into the ear of the other person. I have flashes of an apple tree with dozens of ladybugs crawling from under the bark. The meadow wakes up with a storm of ladybugs, flying off blades of grass and gliding toward me like flower blossoms bursting. They enter my mouth, crawl along my clothes, and prickle all over my skin. Someone used to always tell me that a garden with ladybugs is very lucky. They eat aphids and invisible destructions, so I am afraid to destroy them. I pause to make sure not to swallow the ones in my mouth. With measured breaths I inhale tenderly and then exhale to push them out like bubbles of orange fire. They circle me and return to the meadow, leaving me to wonder where I dropped the cell phone and if I am still connected to the other person on the line.

The Medium Speaks of Birds

I.
Two velvet antlers,
        crown of young buck,
aglow with sunset.
They usher us into
        the golden hour,

toward thick grass
outside the old abbey's entrance,
where he grazes until
        our startling car doors
            close. My friend Heidi and I accept him
as a sign

of good hunting,
of spirits welcoming us,
of an electric witching hour.
        When the whitetail spooks
toward the graveyard,

he also trots away
        from the highway and vineyard,
then leaps
        over barbwire,
into the eventual woods

that will shelter him.
We ask for the same—
        protection inside

the abbey, where they say
        harm and curses
                dwell within
the shadows.

II.
On the ghost hunt, in the abbey's basement,
our hosts invite the dead
to wake up motion sensors,
to knock, and to manifest.
We're seeking scraps
of disembodied voices that echo
on frequencies we can't hear.
We're recording answers on playback.

The two mediums guide us toward
long bouts of silence
in pitch dark rooms
where monks and nuns slept
with secrets. In the large chapel
they sit next to us in creaky church pews.
The mediums take turns calling questions
into the modest rooms,
decorated with lone crosses
above wrought iron beds.
Everyone holds their breath and listens
with their whole body. I'm amused but
take them as a grain of salt.

III.

We are the second group to enter the basement,
and we listen to the medium greeting any spirits
who wish to communicate. He calls out appearing
visions and tells us to speak if any fit within us.

"I see fish. A bucket of fish. Maybe two people fishing together."
(Miss.)

"I see a sugar skull. Maybe it's a tattoo? Maybe it's on a T-shirt."
(Miss.)

"I see . . . an avocado?"   (Hit.)

"This speaks to me," I hear myself say. The others shift to look
toward my voice.

"Did you recently lose someone?"   (Hit.)

"Was it your father?"   (Hit.)

"How long ago?"   (Four months.)

The curl of question mark after he says "avocado"
speaks to me like my father's presence. The motion sensor
    disrupts
the emptiness down the hall. The nervous energy builds
and the medium turns attention toward the arrival
of a dark spirit
he has encountered here before.

After the session ends, I hold out
my leather sugar skull notebook to the medium and Heidi.
I reveal the poem inside
that I wrote about my father and avocados.

IV.

We're doing EVP work in the vault where they kept the bodies
when the ground was too frozen to dig. Atmosphere chills
to the touch. The second medium refuses to enter, drawn away
from the group. He asks for a volunteer and I follow, leaning
    into fear.
We stop in a hallway, between the crematorium and what he
    calls
the potato room. On a doorway tired Halloween decorations
    hang
from the last time the abbey held a haunted house. After
    establishing me as
the man who lost his father, he offers condolences and we
    begin—

V.

"I see your dad speechless. He can't talk and keeps grabbing at
his throat." (Hit.)

"I see the word 'fall.' It ended him but not from a great height."
(Hit.)

"I see a balloon; a hot air balloon."   (Miss.)

"Have you seen a strange new bird? Maybe it flew into your
house?" (Miss.)

"Did he die in February?"   (Hit.)

"Have there been any birds on your window sill?"   (Miss.)

"Okay. Look for it in the next day or so. You'll see."   (. . .)

"I am seeing two sisters."   (I have two.)

"Not them. Do you know any other sisters?" (Maybe.)

"Your father will meddle for the next few months. Maybe November
or December."   (. . .)

You can always speak to him if you like. He is listening."   (Thank you.)

"Nineteen or twenty-one?" (Nineteen. Hit.)

VI.
Wrapped in darkness, he explains, "When the dead are recent,
they can go back and forth through the door between two lands."
We exit the basement and rejoin the larger group. I wonder
if I fed him any cues. Heidi asks if I am okay.

VII.
In the 4:00 a.m. exhaustion,
        after seeking clues in empty bedrooms,
            the echoing gymnasium, and the cemetery
            on the far side of the property,
        always holding gizmos and recorders,
I drive home and Heidi dozes, trying to
        resist her heavy eyelids.

Before she sleeps
I keep asking what really happened.
     Am I conflating? Am I looking for signs
     that aren't there? Am I letting grief
     overtake me? She simply answers,
"I was there and something happened."

     Now, alone in the car while she sleeps,
         I drive east and back to Pueblo.
I'm left to work through the foggy messages
     of the mediums and ghosts
from somewhere too vivid to be dream.

The House of Bees

My father's childhood home
was condemned a few years before.
Looking at the simple house, above us
on the slight hill, I wanted to enter, except
my tía stopped me, pointing to
the home now alive with wasps
and bees, humming in and out,
returning it to the humid mountains.
My father told me he used to
send $35 a month to help
pay the mortgage when he was in the Army.
What I want to do, from the mainland,
is to let the insects keep the house
safe from extinction and to welcome the lizards
that scamper along walls and ceilings, so my dad has
a homecoming in Lajas, inside
the house of bees, with hives
built up in every corner, where ant colonies
climb from the ground
in the shape of the ancestors
my father swore they all saw
watching them in his childhood nights.

The Migratory Patterns of Chupacabras

You first sucked goats dry
through Puerto Rican countryside,

stared us down with red, oval eyes,
before escaping into starless nights.

The unknown lights accompany you in Chilean skies
to drain llanos of steer into mortis,

to splatter open chicken coops in Venezuela
and Nicaragua, to drink up Mexican shores like Cortes.

Your signature is a puncture wound
on an animal's throat with no signs of struggle.

You are the exsanguinations reported on Univision,
pastoral crime scenes ignored by CNN and *The Today Show*.

In your pursuit, we are left to wonder you as the demon,
gifted with flight, or the pachyderm-skinned dogs

with freakishly long canines and claws,
running from rifle-toting ranchers murdering in Texas.

We keep chasing you like the smoke of rumors
that sends us through Chicago boroughs and back out

to where we might lose your name, a nombre that captures you
in the vanishing between field and horizon.

Dream of the Sun Spirit

The landscape is an infinity of Japanese woodblocks, and when I look behind the sun and under one of its thick, red rays, I find the globe-shaped creature. Like several animals spliced together and dipped in the color of lava flow, it animates its bird head to speak flames from opened beak and eyes. Its body suggests cogs, sprockets, and ancient gears beneath. I can't see its legs but its arms point and swim in the air. It nourishes the lush hills and valleys out of my reach. I blink too long and it vanishes back into the sun. When I describe what I saw to an old man that night, he scolds me for losing it before receiving the map made of sunlight. I feel foolish and empty-handed until I remember the spirit still sauntering inside my head.

Grandpa Money

My dad collected coins.
He ordered limited editions and all
state and national park quarters.
He especially loved change
from the Denver Mint.

He gave me
a gold Sacajawea to have
when he asked for it
on his deathbed,
something we never got to do.

He handed out
two-dollar bills
to my daughters and my nieces
and called it
Grandpa Money.

Ever since he's passed,
we are finding
old wheat pennies
in odd places, Lincoln faceup
and always unclaimed.

My mom and sisters believe
he leaves them
on our nightstands, window
ledges, and tabletops
for safe passage later on.

We accept his bread crumbs
from the afterlife,
as reminders that
we are together now
and lucky to be here.

Inside My Black Sugar Skull Notebook

I am newly-scribed pages,
ascending past
raw data drops and boulevards of memory
                                    I don't control. I comb
                                    through
                                    handwriting

harsh like gritas.
                My mother grieves more than I ever will, yet
                I hold a heavy stance

        before the portrait of
        her husband, my father, which once fell
        off the wall

when she was thinking his name. I suggest she talks
out loud to him. She doesn't want
        her own painting when
        it's time for their reunion.

                                    After describing my
                                    dreams, someone asks
                                    more than once if I think

                my dad extraterrestrial,
                        instructing me to follow him into
the recesses,

like the realtor I knew in New Mexico who found
                                    a glistening, purple stone
                                    hiking

through the Sandia Mountains. He told me it was
                                    from the planet Neptune
                                    and then
                    spoke of past lives.

Remember: All darkness looks alive.

Let—
            the stone,
            the father,
            the mother,
            the dream
                                    send us to pursue the
                                    house of
                                    questions, shaped
                        as a sugar skull,
                        assembled from
animated bodies hanging as the twists and sizzling
bends of neon lights.

Dream of Synchronicity

Everyone drinks and clinks glasses in the hotel bar, spilling
into the lobby. I'm cornered and sorting through a box of lost
earrings, trying for a matching pair. I give up when I find the
pinball machine that everyone says unlocks time travel. With
a stack of quarters, I'm tapping flipper buttons and sending
the ball into bumpers. I'm fighting pings of gravity. I'm tilting
the machine to keep the ball alive on the playfield. The display
is a black monolith that doesn't keep score. Then it's after
school and I'm walking through my high school's parking lot.
A student next to me says, "I'm not sure you're supposed to
be here, man." I nod to him, unsure if he means 1999 or 2019.
Before I can ascertain how it works, I'm standing before the
pinball machine again, now on a cold, morning beach that
might be on a distant moon. The waves casually murmur on
about synchronicity.

One Year Later

I.
At the end of the beautiful war movie
the screen goes dark,
except for a dedication
to the director's grandfather,
who survived WWI.
I leave the theater, crying
uncontrollably. My friends understand but
look away. I sob
alone in my car
and dwell on the melancholy
of Dad's survival
stories, hopeful that the wars within him
are finally resting,
even if he is not.

II.
He is everywhere
like lucky pennies, always heads up.
We are wondering Dad
a trickster and if we somehow
kicked him awake.
When we sense him
we do not tremble
or turn away.

III.
Mom tells us she found Pop

in bed, during the witching hour.
When she asked him if he
was going to work, Dad told her
he didn't have to leave
until 5:30. She keeps insisting
it just felt too real. He vanished
when she climbed
out of bed
to make their coffee.

IV.

My sister's home security footage
records orbs and streaks
of light manifesting
in her kitchen and living room.
In one clip several orbs appear
around my father's
favorite hat. She invites him
to talk to her. We obsess over
her orb videos, seeking signs
but knowing
deep down
that they are all just dust.

V.

After a snowstorm, the neighbor,
also named Jose, clears
the snow from my mom's walk and driveway.
Mom thanks him, and Jose insists
her husband, Mr. Morales, told him
to help. My mom tries to ask Jose
when this happened, but it's unclear.

A few days later, after
another accumulation, a GI living
a few doors down
clears the snow and gives Mom
the same kindness.

VI.
On Groundhog Day
the military cemetery
is almost empty,
and we apologize
for forgetting flowers.
His epitaph, chiseled
in the cold, stone slab, keeps
what feels holy.
His response waits for
each question we have—
"When they call
to me, I will
answer them."

Excerpt from
Shit My Puerto Rican Father Said

On a rainy day, before leaving for school, my mom asked, "Juancito, do you need an umbrella?" Before I could, my father answered for me, "Ah, Maria, he don't need no stinkin' umbrella because he's tough. T-O-F. TOF!" I remember wondering if he would spell out the whole word or not.

My Mother's Dreams

*

When I first describe my dreams, Mom asks why doesn't Dad visit her too? I don't know how to answer that or how she swears that she's heard him sneeze twice and once heard him call, "Mari, Mari, Mari!" from somewhere upstairs. When she searches, her house remains empty.

*

When Dad finally comes to her, Mom stands in between two swimming pools, in an old gymnasium full of shadows. The water is too dark to see the bottom. My father says something and dives into the pool to the left. She reminds me that he couldn't swim when he was alive. Staring down and waiting for him to surface, her terror forms as a lump in her throat. If I could have the moment again, I would tell her how we are different in dreams, that maybe he was underwater and discovering that he could now swim.

*

In Mom's final recurring dream, she's in bed and Dad is getting up to check on a noise downstairs. He faces away from her and she touches his back. He is cold. Mom usually calls it a nightmare because she wants to see his face so bad. She asks if she should get a new mattress, and I'm confused until it's explained that she's had the same mattress for forty years. Maybe because I watch too many horror movies, maybe because I imagine him replaced by a demon, or maybe because he'll be wearing his embalmed face, I change the subject back to her maybe buying a new mattress could help. I imagine them in simple comfort, together again on the back porch or walking around Quail Lake, but I stop myself because it is her dream, not mine.

Actualization Principle

At Lago Muerte the fishermen calmly cast out their lines,
reeling in very tiny fish. I felt out of place because I forgot my
pole. When I looked closer, the lake was an empty plain filled
with dried logs and rocks. I could barely make out the line
where the waves once lapped. One of the fishermen turned to
me. "This is an impossible feeling," he said as he tugged another
glistening one out of the lake. The fish tried to breathe and
stared past me. "Everything is nonsense, but you can't help
but feel lucky." He resumed fishing. Afraid of being hooked by
one of them, I backed up. I started telling them about the time
I hooked my thumb all the way through, but they stopped me
because I had already told them.

Looking for Duende

My parents had a sprinkler
that sputtered water whenever
the tap was off, and mom surprised me
when she casually said
duende was watering the backyard again.
I heard duende as Lorca's captured inspiration
in college. I asked how to translate it
into English, and my parents couldn't,
settling on "the mischief of a goblin."
Mom added that it's like
the movie with small green gremlins terrorizing
the Pennsylvania town
during Christmas.
When I left home,
sent out to find duende,
the muse gifted deep wells of dream,
podcasts about skinwalkers and tricksters
orchestrating mischief, winds singing
through remote woods
to echo like ocean waves.
I didn't know I first encountered duende
in the *Looney Tunes* cartoon
where Bugs Bunny saves
the B-52 bomber from the small saboteur
and William Shatner's *Twilight Zone* plane ride,
watching monsters dismantle
the engine before flying into the lightning
and leaving him in lunacy.

Duende coaxed me to pedal faster
on my childhood's rickety bike,
to follow shadows mistaken
for witches, to welcome déjà vu
on mountain trails I've never hiked before.
I still search beyond Lorca's execution
and mass grave
whenever I study full moon's grief.
I accept the medium's summertime warning
that my dead father has become duende,
promising to meddle
until we safely make it
into the chilly months of
November and December.

Dream of the Mummy

A stranger carried her body under his arm like an umbrella. It
stopped raining when I took her in my arms and he vanished
into the fog. The mummy was a light but powerful woman,
Mother from another time. Her opened eyes were not
interested in revenge for her cursed jewels. Her exposed teeth,
desiccated skin, and muted linens would have haunted my
childhood, but not today. I carried her past landscapes where
compasses go haywire and wildlife ignores us. We stopped.
I rested her on the soft earth, surrounded by the ceremony
of weaved grasses and flowering reeds. Fighting the guilt of
abandoning her, I walked all the back to the city, ready to
answer for the museum's empty sarcophagus, so her people
could welcome her home.

Excerpt from
Shit My Puerto Rican Father Said

*

I arrived late to my niece's birthday party at a Chuck E. Cheese, and I sat across from my pissed-off father, sipping coffee out of a Styrofoam cup. The flashing video games, laughing kids, and subpar pizza wore at his nerves. When I asked him if he was having fun, he looked around to capture the spirit of the moment and replied, "This place is suck."

Magpies, Building a Nest

My mom sits inside the hospice center
talking to the grief counselor
for the first time. She struggles to untangle
her feelings since Dad died a few weeks ago.

She has already asked me,
"Aren't I supposed to get through this by myself?"
But she humors me by going and even dresses up a little
with a knitted, red sweater.

I am outside, trying to read a book,
in a hoodie that makes me feel like a trespasser
on a sunny but chilly spring morning.
When I pace the parking lot, I catch the flicker

of blue on wings, long tail feathers.
The two magpies chirp back and forth, building
in a tall pine tree. They fly away for short durations
to collect. One stick at a time, they assemble,

and I think about how I used to dismiss them
as scavengers, pecking at roadkill or stealing shiny trash,
ignoring how their teal and turquoise
glide in harmony with their white and black feathers.

After the appointment, I point them out and Mom nods.
"Que bella," she adds, even though she's busy
processing the uncomfortable hour
just shared with the grief counselor.

It is quiet between us, except for the unassuming song
of the magpies, still weaving together their nest.
She's not persuaded, but agrees to return
in two weeks. I am surprised and thinking about

my own therapy and when we will talk about
getting rid of Dad's old clothes. I ask her when she thinks
the magpies will lay their eggs. She doesn't answer.
Instead, Mom reminds me that Dad

used to say, "Life can be rough, but it's still beautiful anyway."
When she tells me that, it's much prettier to hear in Spanish.

Boricua Economics

The yellow mutt cornered the iguana against
a chain link fence,
tightening its perimeter,
just out of reach of the iguana's tail
that could snap off
blood and skin. The dog bared its teeth
until the lizard squeezed under
to escape into the jungle's matching green.
The dog lost interest
and left me to wonder
which animal capture the island's
limbo of territory status,
prosperity overgrown in recession jungles?
I looked into the sky
at the mainland vultures, looming
like foreclosures and Wall Street hedge funds,
before deciding
both live here, feeling something
that lies between
desire and defiance.

Excerpt from
Shit My Puerto Rican Father Said

*

Every time Mama would say, "Maybe we should get a dog," Dad would tell her, "If you want a dog, I can bark."

Bury Me in a Guayabera

The shirts are tradition—
Dad handed me the mail order catalog and asked
what I wanted. I declined polyester pants but
always humored him by picking a guayabera
that would arrive six to eight weeks later
in a stuffed Haband envelope. I didn't wear them much
until I was older, but I always felt safe
knowing they hung in the closet.

Pop wore polo shirts and khakis or his dark-blue suit
for church, so we always noticed when
he broke out his guayaberas
with pressed slacks and polished wingtips,
reminding me how
my sister used to always say
he was more fun when he was Catholic.

Mom asked me to take
whatever I wanted from my father's closet.
I took two cans of shoe polish, a stack
of handkerchiefs, and his three guayaberas—
the two white ones with inlay I was
too heavy to wear before
and a sky blue one, just like his eyes.

And now I look to the mirror and admire
each bold button, the two embroidered stripes
dancing down the chest

like festive snakes, climbing over
the pockets, ready for daily ceremonies
that tell the world—
bury me in a guayabera,
shirt of my forebearers,
or better yet, dress me in this one,
cremate me, and then spread me
wherever I seemed
most happy.

Dad Watching *Jackass*

He was mostly gruff, with PTSD
and work shifts dragging behind him, but there were days
when I discovered him watching MTV's *Jackass*—
morons thrown around by a bull in heat,
snapping mouse traps on nipples and crotches,
and taking turns in exploding porta potties.
My dad always called them "dumb sons-of-bitches,"
cackling to tears when they raced grocery carts
into brick walls and launched themselves with giant slingshots
into thorny thickets. He rode the wave
of slapstick, with the same howls that I can't hold back
watching fail videos that speak the international language of
a ball smacking someone in the face.

I watch *AFV* and *Fail Army* in his honor. I seek the balance
of cute animals, childhood mishaps, and adult tantrums
that makes my whole body laugh. I keep searching for
the late-night movie Dad saw on Univision, where
a man farted whenever he saw a gun. I remember my father in tears
taking me scene-by-scene through every fart—
the bank robbery, the car heist, and the track meet
where even the calm before the starting gun
is interrupted by a man's flatulence. I don't know how it ends because
Dad couldn't stop laughing, but I take comfort there is
a film out there, committed to conjuring
our twelve-year-old selves back
and all the jackasses offering themselves up for those
who don't get to laugh enough in this life.

"20,000 Pallets of Bottled Water Left Untouched in Storm-Ravaged Puerto Rico"

September 20, 2018

On a runway in Celba, under blue tarps pulled taut,
FEMA's water shipment still sits, one year after Maria.
Against a backdrop of the people boiling river water,
the agency apologizes for *distribution issues*,
officials promising to test each bottle,
though everyone knows it's as foul as their island support.
In the gaze of the aerial shots—pallet after pallet—stretching out
like a crumbled runway, the tallies of the dead jump from
64 to 3,000, and
the mainland president tweets congratulations to all
on a *job well done*. The island is a dry throat,
a voice in the eye of the aftermath, hissing words
unspoken elsewhere: *commonwealth, statehood, independence?*

Dream of the Widow

We gather in a lush backyard with a menagerie of old friends, as if to say, This is your life. When the widow approaches, she wraps me in a strong hug. She whispers, "I'm so sorry you lost him," and I try to give her condolences for her husband who passed a few months ago, except I'm tongue-tied. I want her to know I meant to visit sooner, I think of her children, and I don't even know how he died. She interrupts with "I know," telling me I am forgiven. I tell the widow out loud, "I wish I was a better friend to you." She waves it off, and we rejoin our friends. I scan everyone's faces, accepting my father and her husband's absence. Everyone looks to the widow. When she nods, they reveal small memories in their open palms, like pebbles from outlying shores and mountaintops. She invites me to collect them all.

Excerpt from
Shit My Puerto Rican Father Said

*

On vacation we ordered breakfast at a mom-and-pop restaurant in Ecuador. Dad helped time pass with his irritation: "Now we need to wait for them to finish milking the goddamn cow." A little later, he added, "They caught the chicken and now they're shaking out the eggs." At the end of the meal, just like he did at every other restaurant, he smacked his lips in satisfaction and declared, "Not bad."

Dear Mama

Whenever Dad fell asleep reading
The Army Times or his Bible
with the broken spine, his glasses
threatened to fall off his nose.
He also dozed with arms folded
through ball games, listening to innings
top to bottom. Forgive me for overlooking—
you telling him to lean back
and how he always complied, adrift
on closed eyes and a light snore.

Dream of the Magic Coat

I wander the night made of many fragments that assemble into a flea market full of my students. The most important object is the old coat I am wearing. Someone declares it magic. Everyone has advice on what to do with its powers. Someone references *Harry Potter* and they gasp disappointment when I confess I have never read or watched it. They call me unworthy because I still don't know how to unlock its powers. The coat feels big so I wonder if I could alter the sleeves. I appreciate its drab brown and ancient buttons and then make the wish to disappear back into night's mosaic, twinkling to life with ice and fire.

Dream of the Devil on Instant Messenger

His username is MALE and his messages are turquoise. Mine
are red. We chat with the kindness of old friends. Then I am
in my father's body, in a helicopter over the jungle near Binh
Khe. I blink in the sun's glare to see a giant mountain of sugar,
covered with ants. Now my back is to the colonial church,
surrounded by a labyrinth of stucco walls and rice paddies.
I can't tell if it's a villager or not; either way, I am assumed a
threat. When an American soldier approaches, I hop a wall and
hide deeper in the labyrinth. Terror is my dark hair sticking up
to give away my location. I'm surprised by another American,
smoking a cigarette across from me. Tobacco fibers pop tiny
infernos when his eyes detect mine. I place my finger to my
lips, and he replies by walking straight through me. He speaks
with his comrades in overlapping voices on the other side. I'm
drowning—the fear of duty, the fear of sacrifice. Then I'm back
in my body, and the Devil has left the chat. I'm leaning in front
of the blank screen on elbows pointed like knives. My mother
tells me it couldn't be the Devil because people who talk to him
are always scared.

Aubade

This is for you, driving down at 4 a.m.
with your bass bumpin', annoying
the pillow bound and daring
dogs to howl up my street. Are you waking
yourself to the subwoofer's rattle of music
or are you homebound after a night
mourned like a crushed but unfinished
cigarette? Maybe, later on, I'll stand
in the grocery store line with you
without knowing you were the one
awake when I was an insomniac, grading papers
in a cold kitchen, wanting
my coffee still trembling hot
without a sunrise in sight.

If the Octopus Dreams

In the viral video the octopus sleeps in the black, along the top
of the water, suctioned to her tank's glass walls. Her reflection
slowly ripples. At first she's a placated white, like pristine
glaciers that have avoided pollution. The texture roughens—
spiky as the fragile coral reef that breathes brown, yellow, and
gray. When the head twitches she clouds into the red, purple,
and black until transitioning to a gray that surrenders to
yellow. Her head and eyes waver but remain shut. Somewhere
in its dancing colors, I witness a Martian landscape appear,
a cloud of harsh storm, and then back to the peaceful swivel
and drift of clouds that bounce on the water's surface. The
scientists report it unlikely to be octopus dreams, but instead
of worrying, I accept all invitations to be submerged.

Life Is a Dream, Then You Wake Up

After Enrique Chagoya

The pressed bark from the sacred tree becomes amate paper,
breathing codices and dreaming of a blue head that dominates a
    sienna landscape.
Faded tears smudge the white background.

The bald head, juxtaposed over two others, creates a blurry drift.
One is a Mayan god's skull, baring teeth and eyes doubled as
    targets.
The other two are incomplete phrenologies with solid and dotted
    eyes,
out of sync and barely contained by thick-lined craniums
surrounded by emphasis lines. These faces attract images
    haunting around—

the Ninja Turtle skull with dazed eyes, red and blue nervous
    system
tiptoeing. A disembodied hand, with bone exposed from wrist,
drops a paintbrush toward a miniature warrior's skeleton.
Warrior draws arrow
to bow, preparing to shoot from ground up. Five targets line the
    middle horizon,

but does the warrior aim at the Illuminati triangle, meant to be
    the skull's nasal cavity,
or the stray eye with a heavy eyelid in the top right corner?

Coaxed inside the head's many faces, we wake up. Our closed
    eyes dream
and hands brush across the amate paper. We are touching skin
from pre-contact times, in the half-seen jungle that feeds
    sacred trees,
branches stirring above in the heavens
and roots searching the dark, rich earth.

Excerpt from
Shit My Puerto Rican Father Said

*

During a friend's visit, my father was watering the front lawn
with the hose and wearing a white tank top that showed faded
tattoos and shrapnel wounds on his arms and shoulders. When
my intimidated friend greeted my father, Pop started and
ended the conversation with, "Hey! Life's a bitch, ah?" Before
entering the house, the only thing left for my friend to do was
to politely agree.

Veterans Day Weekend

It's the start of Veterans Day weekend. Fifty-eight degrees. No wind.
I expect to get lost but instantly find your tombstone, now
surrounded by green. The blades yellow along the tips.
There's a stained line along the white marble from a Weedwacker.
You don't mind. I feel naive thinking you hear me, among
the other servicemen and women. I'm trying to see Mom
as much as I can, but it never feels like enough. She needs you
more than saying "I miss you" can convey. The last time I saw you
your eyes carried worry about my stress and weight, so I need you to know
that I'm okay. Thank you for the cricket and small-dotted beetle
on your marker. Life going on around you,
you're finally ready to stop meddling.

Commendations

To whom it may concern,

Please accept this
as proof that my father,
Jose Morales Lugo,
served as an ROTC instructor
at the University of Iowa
for three years, 1978 to 1981,
before retiring from the US Army
even if it is unofficial.

In the year I was born
he received commendations
for teaching until expunged
thirty-eight years later
because of the clerical error
that switched
his social security number
with his commanding officer's.
Pop called the Army, VA,
the CO's last known number,
and university offices.
We filled out forms
to right the wrong.

After Dad's death
I promised to raise hell until
they fixed his record.
Before I could, Mom told me
it didn't matter anymore,
so my last step is
to help her
keep his files, certificates,
and medals
in the order that Pop
assembled them.

Thank you
for helping us
put it all to rest.

Dream of the Flooded Bathroom

In the basement bathroom of my parent's house, all the pipes
shuddered just before sink, toilet, and shower erupted with
water. I threw towels on the floor, then worked the plunger
to no avail. I suddenly heard my father to my left, cussing his
favorite chain of hostias and carajos. He sliced a mop through
the water and complained how the rust-colored water probably
meant the kitchen would also overflow. I tried to send him
away, but he became a younger, stubborn version of himself:
"Not this time, Son." Unburdened, I worked beside my father,
until the water met its high mark and then started to subside.

Of Deer, or Los Venados

Mom smiles when the deer,
los venados, hop the chain link
and graze in her backyard,
even when they feed on
the peach trees and lilacs.
There's usually three does
and one buck with a broken antler
who rest in the shade. Once,
she stood two feet away,
on the back porch, but could not
bring herself closer. We want the buck
to be you, Pop, telling Mom
she is not alone. Meanwhile, I am
forty miles away from her
and mixed up in dreams,
which makes me a distant constellation.
I never call enough so I'm asking
your visits to transcend
into dreamscape, where Mom
can cup her hands
to your ear and whisper
questions she's been
needing to ask you.
Your horns branching
into glowing sky.

Dream of Acceptance

The woman from my past told me / she had upsetting news. I
braced myself // and she described how the EMTs, who worked
on my father, / learned from the mistakes they made on him. //
They learned how to decrease / the blood pressure for someone
who suffered / a fall just like Pop's. The stranger would survive.
// I remained stoic, thanked her, and walked outside, / ready
for anger to overtake me. // Instead, I stood in the forest with
firs that rose higher than / heaven, bathed in morning sunlight.
It emanated white // between the trunks. I smiled because, for
a minute, I felt my father / alive again because of the stranger's
survival. // The light brightened and hummed all around / until
I couldn't see anything at all.

Excerpt from
Shit My Puerto Rican Father Said

*

Every time I called my parents I eased into speaking Spanish
with my mom for a while. I got comfortable, she taught me
new words, and she corrected me when I stumbled. When she
passed the phone to my father he greeted me with "What's up,
Papo?" and chitchatted sports and talked to me in English. I
asked him how he was feeling. He always answered, "I'm cool,
baby. I'm cool."

Dream of the Bird Tattoo

After the medium told me a strange bird would visit me, I
obsessed over every sparrow and finch in our yard, including
one that perched outside the kitchen window, head tilted in
curiosity. The yellow prairie warbler chased moths around the
neighbor's red maple. I counted Mississippi kites whistling
high above, green hummingbirds flitting through to nourish on
our succulents, and crows dogfighting with red-tailed hawks.
Every bird reminded me of avian populations in decline, but
they ignored my need for personal prophecy. A few nights later,
when my eyes closed, my deceased father stood before me with
face obscured. His shoulder tattoo of la golondrina stirred.
Then the swallow climbed off his shoulder as a green phoenix
made of neon light. It shook its wings and told me, "This is the
bird you are looking for," before flying out of the dream and
waking me, just like sunrise.

Acknowledgments

I started writing and drafting some of the sueñitos and poems in this book twenty years ago, so I'm happy the little dreams found their home in this book. Thank you to David Keplinger for introducing me to Charles Simic and for advising me to write my dreams.

Whether through emails, social media, texts, or phone calls, I couldn't have done this without the talented poets, artists, and writers who offered support, conversation, and feedback: Millicent Accardi, Francisco Aragón, Byron Aspaas, Sandra Beasley, Jessica Boehman, David Campos, Rigoberto González, Steven Hayward, Jonathan Bohr Heinen, Maria Melendez Kelson, Alysse Kathleen McCanna, José Antonio Rodriguez, Darci Schummer, and Klint Skelly. Thank you to Andrew Jones for talking ghosts, UFOs, cryptids, *X-Files*, creation, and process as I worked through this book with your album *Pueblo* on repeat. Thank you to the workshops, organizations, and writing conferences that gave me inspiration and time to write, including, but not limited to, CantoMundo, Letras Latinas, Macondo, SOMOS, Longleaf Writers Conference, and Jackson Hole Writers Conference. Thank you also to Andrea, Mike, and everyone at Lighthouse Writers, whose community gave me time to write at the Grand Lake Writing Retreat multiple times.

Many thanks to the hardworking editors of the following magazines, journals, and anthologies, where many of these poems originally appeared, sometimes in different versions: *Acentos Review, The Big Other, BreakBeat Poets Volume 4: Latinext, Chachalaca Review, Collateral, Crazyhorse, Green Mountains Review, The Laurel Review, Pank, Poetry, Salamander, South Dakota Review, Speculative Futures, Split This Rock Poetry Database, Sugar House Review, terrain.org,* and *Water~Stone Review.*

Gratitude to my students, who were in class with me when I first drafted poems; to Leticia and Trisha; to my colleagues; and to CSU Pueblo: thank you to my beautiful campus community for so many years. To my Colorado College students and colleagues: thank you for making me feel so welcomed and supported.

To my therapist, Daphyne, who worked with me through grief and life's challenges. Thanks for sitting at the pond with me, where we admired the geese and ducks, and for helping to channel it into my poetry. To Elise and Mari, who both believed in this book from the start and talked through synchronicities, coincidences, and dreamscapes with me too.

Gratitude to our Pueblo family for always being there for us; gratitude to Sean, Jitka, Muck, Kelsea, Alex, Sarah, Mike C., and all the running folk, who helped me discover this new challenge that helps my mental health; and gratitude to Heidi for adventuring into the abbey with me and confirming what actually happened.

Love and gratitude to my family, who gave me the courage, support, and wisdom to navigate grief, and for helping me remember to laugh and smile with all the great stories about Dad—Carrie, Alyssa, Ritchie, Richard, Esther, Morgan, Andrés, Ronan, Elise, Syd, Regan, Eric, Glenn, Rosita, Thais, Gwyneth, Rafa, Carmen, Victor, Hans, Alex, Erin, Katie, Enrique, y toda la familia en Ecuador and PR. To our mother, Maria, who taught me strength and the mantra I'll never forget: Poco a poco.

To my wife, Patti—thank you for being my editor, my love, and my light. Thank you for waiting in the February cold so we could see Gregory Alan Isakov play immediately after Pop's wake, and for holding my hand in the dark, where I could weep and get lost with you in the hauntingly beautiful music.